A NIGERIAN AMERICAN
FAMILY & THE U.S

JUSTICE SYSTEM

ARBITRARY PROSECUTION

MR. CLIFFORD UBANI

When federal agents knock on his door, the life Clifford Ubani has built with his family in America changes forever.

He built this life with dreams but no illusions. When he came to Houston, Clifford's cousin greeted him with a warning: These white people don't like you; they hated you the moment you set foot into their country.

Born in Abia, Nigeria, Clifford worked from a young age to support his family and pursue his education before travelling to America to pursue further opportunities. He played by the rules, a dedicated student studying criminal justice. Hoping to change the system from the inside, he gained a greater understanding of both sides of the law. America is where Clifford reunited with the love of his life under surprising circumstances and raised a special family.

A friend to other Africans and both black and white Americans, he gained a reputation as a probation officer whose training and background helped to connect the dots in difficult cases. Still, as a black officer, he got praise while others got the promotions. And after he leaves the probation department to become an entrepreneur, the dream is attacked: Clifford is indicted on multiple accounts of fraud and conspiracy.

His confidence in justice is quickly shaken when it becomes apparent that the true conspiracy lies behind his arrest and prosecution—an attempt to punish a black man for doing well.

In a system where African Americans are disproportionately represented, where cursory and inaccurate processes can lead to undervalued lives ruined by wrongful conviction, he prepares to fight every step of the way for what he knows is right.

A Nigerian American Family and the U.S. Justice System is the searing true story of American racism from an African perspective, an insider's look at how so-called justice can betray its own, and a story of hope, love, and survival.

Equal justice under the law is not merely a caption on the facade of the Supreme Court building, it is perhaps the most inspiring ideal of our society.

It is one of the ends for which our entire legal system exists... it is fundamental that justice should be the same, in substance and availability, without regard for economic status

LEWIS POWEL JR.

TABLE OF CONTENTS

PROLOGUE

❧

No sooner had I dropped the phone than I heard a knock on the door. I looked back, and my wife and kids were still there, crying profusely. The knock came again, and so I shifted to the door.

"Good evening, Mr. Clifford Ubani. I am Federal Agent Ross," the officer leading the raid announced immediately upon entering my house.

"Good evening Officer, Ross," I replied, trying hard to hide the nervousness in my voice.

"We are here to bring you in and to search your property," he continued, displaying a search and arrest warrant to my face. "Come with me, Mr. Clifford, while the officers do their job."

I nodded and followed him. Several officers walked past us into the house as we made our way toward the vehicles parked outside my house.

Now, I was starting to get scared. I was sure my lawyer would be cooking something up, but all the same, I felt so terrified that it surprised me despite my preparations. I still believed in justice, so I was not very bothered. As I was driven out of the neighborhood, I could see my wife and kids standing on the porch, watching.

I was taken to the FBI office and kept in a waiting room.

Chapter One
THE BEGINNING

I was not sure if I was scared or just nervous; the two sounded different but seemed the same to me, especially on a day like this. While I waited for the big bird, one thought quickly choked my excitement: What if it never came? Would they return every payment I'd made or call for another plane? These were thoughts that would chip in every now and then during my one-hour wait at the Murtala Muhammed Airport, Ikeja, Lagos. While I waited, many things caught my attention and also entertained me. One was the busyness in the arrival and departure halls. Another was the voice sending out loud instructions over speakers that were in almost every corner of the large halls. Occasionally, my mind wandered off back home. I thought about my siblings, what they were doing right now at the village. I was missing them already, but they were going to miss me too and more importantly, they would be proud of me.

I thought about my greatest inspiration, my mother. I missed her the most, to be honest. My face turned gloomy quickly when I reminded myself of the fact that I would never see her again, no, not in this life, perhaps in dreams. It saddened me more that she was not around to witness today, to see how I had fought and survived, to see how I had managed not to give up even after all odds. I remember when I used to wonder if I should be grateful for growing up without a mother, but no doubt, I was young and foolish those times. At a very tender age, I had become strong and independent and wise enough to live life even at its cruel peak and also man up to assist my siblings, but then, I later figured I would have been greater than this if my mother was still alive. Perhaps I would not have gone through so many troubles to achieve one of the many goals I have in life.

My nostalgic session came to an end when more individuals trooped into the hall. My mind bounced back into the room, and I continued to enjoy the view before me. Meanwhile, the anxiousness and nervousness, mixed with a little pinch of fear, all returned visibly to my face. I left my home town for Lagos the previous day, but I arrived in the city late at night due to the severe breakdown of the bus I boarded. We had to wait for three hours until the bus was fixed. Eventually, I arrived Lagos. My flight was scheduled for the next day. I had a hard time sleeping and resting my head. When morning came, I was already up and ready, and so I arrived the airport exactly thirty-five minutes before 8:00 AM, only to discover that my flight had been delayed for an hour. I was left alone with my luggage and thoughts until someone spoke to me:

"First time traveling?"

I turned my head to the left to see a woman who, though agile, would be as old or older than my mother if she were still alive.

"Yes madam, it is my first time," I replied, smiling sheepishly. Was it so obvious? I wondered.

"Don't be scared, son. That is how it is for first timers, but it will be fine."

At first, I was somehow moved to come closer to this strange woman; her last word was like a soothing promise to my unstable heart, like a pain reliever for my aching knees.

"Thank you, madam."

Before I knew it, I was narrating all of my ordeals since I became an orphan, the different hardship I went through until I finally got here today. In the end, she was moved, no doubt. I was not really after the compassion and attention, but in some way, I felt drawn to the woman. She was surprised and also impressed at how I could survive, how I never let go of my dreams no matter the setbacks I encountered. She told me I was bound for a settled and bright future if I continued my striving and did not give in to any form of distraction. To be honest, I enjoyed talking to the woman and was even more surprised when I learned we were waiting for the same flight and also bound for the same destination.

As we talked on, I never forgot to pay close attention to the instructions being spilled out over the speakers so when the plane we were waiting for arrived, I was quick to hear a the news. As we worked our way into the plane, my mind sang me songs of home and I was gloomy again, but I comported myself; it was not like it was going to be the last time I would be seeing my family. But what if it was? This new, evil thought I nursed topped the fear I already has in mind about planes— of a crash especially. As far as accidents were concerned, it was rare for anyone to survive plane crashes and even if they did, they would be in a very bad state. But I quickly waved away the thought.

Once comfortably tucked inside the plane, I shut my eyes and bowed my head to pray. One of the things I learned from home, from my mother. At a very young age, my mother had taught my siblings and I about God and at the same time, she made us commit our lives to him. We never forgot to pray, even after our mother left us. After I prayed in the plane, I raised my head to see the same woman from the airport now occupying the seat next to mine. I smiled and bowed my head slightly, and she nodded in return with the warmest smile I've ever seen. She must have seen through the fake smile to notice that I was afraid.

"You're scared now, right?" she asked, looking into my eyes. "I can see you are no longer eager to be on the plane," she added.

I smiled again and blushed. Truth be told, I was not anxious anymore; the thoughts about plane crashes had returned, stronger and scary now.

"Yes ma, I guess I'm just scared now," I replied, my gaze fixed squarely on my brown leather shoe.

The strange woman laughed softly but quickly put her hand on mine. "It is going to be fine, son, you just keep calm."

I wanted to cry and then hug her. Her touch and voice calmed me in some sort of strange way; the more we interacted, the more I remembered my mother. Had I missed my mother's love so much that I wanted to follow this woman to her home?

"Besides, you' need to do more than just staring at the floor; you need to look out of the window. There's a lot you need to see, child."

By now, the plane was out on the tarmac and speeding along the runway. Earlier, we had been instructed to fasten our belts. Then the vibration started; I could feel my body easing into the tension as the plane ran along the long black road. Then another instruction was issued: we should prepare for take-off. I shut my eyes the second time as I felt my body starting to pull backward with a force stronger than gravity. Then everything went back to normal.

I raised my head slowly and turned to look out the window, and when I did, a new spark ignited deep down inside me. The spark escalated into a warm fire that burnt through my eyes as I remained fixed. I watched as we hovered above many rusty brown rooftops. Only new rooftops stood out from above by their easily spotted colors; they were like diamonds amidst stones. As the plane soared higher, everything down there was getting smaller, but still, the beauty was too much. I saw greenery spreading far and wide and then water; it was all just too much for me to behold! At a point, I wanted to say something. I did not know what to say in particular, but I was shocked. "Marvelous" could not describe what I saw down there. I received another surprise from nature once we were up in the clouds. What I saw when I looked further down was exactly like the globe I used to see on my headmaster's table back in my village, but this one was much more real.

I turned back and faced the woman with my eyes welling up with impatient tears of gratitude to God, my mother, my siblings, and to everyone that contributed to this, this success.

"It's a nice view, isn't it?" the woman asked.

"It's beautiful," I replied, wiping away a stubborn tear that had managed to escape down my cheeks regardless of how hard I had tried to fight it back. Throughout the flight, we continued talking. The woman was moved; she was surprised that there were still young people who could face the type of challenges I faced and still manage to raise my head above all odds. I told her about my siblings, my village, my school, my last boss before I decided to travel abroad. In return, she encouraged me more and more with her own story, which I found quite profound and inspirational.

I had fed my eyes quite well while waiting in the airport but now, more things caught my attention on the plane. The flight attendants looked all jovial and smart in their neat uniforms. I couldn't help but admire how beautifully they walked, especially the female ones. Their voices alone could put a little kid to sleep; they were always ready to hear your complaints, answer your requests, and provide for your needs with immediate effect, and they never ceased smiling to passengers. Another thing that caught my attention was the food. The snacks were the type that I have only read about or seen in books; they were available and free. I ate only a little to avoid any unnecessary trouble and besides, I was filled with excitement already.

Occasionally, the pilots announced the remaining time we had had to spend in the air before touchdown. The flight that I expected to be boring and lonely was not—in fact, it was lively and total fun for me, all thanks to the woman next to me. She told me so many things, out of which I grasped a particular story she told me about herself.

She was thirteen then, and innocent about life. She stayed with her aunt. She had to move away from home when her father died and, as custom demands, the widow must be in solitude for a year. So, being the only child, she had to stay with her mother's younger sister. During her stay there, she encountered difficulties, one of which remained evergreen in her memory. She had returned from school on Friday to meet her aunt's husband at home. She greeted him and was walking away when he grabbed her. It was a lost fight and, prevailing over her, he deflowered her that day. His attacks continued for a while until she couldn't take it anymore and so she came clean to her aunt, who flared up at the confession. She was beaten and called a witch for telling lies against her helper and trying to ruin their home. She was later sent packing out of the home, but then, she was with a baby. At last, she raised the boy on her own, and now he is a big man in the foreign country of the whites.

I couldn't help but wonder how hard it must have been for her, having to go through those ugly experiences with her aunt's husband, then having to suffer at the hands of her aunt and be thrown out of the house to survive alone. This story settled in a separate place in my heart. It was indeed a sad one that could have gone worse if the woman had not picked up her pieces and continued the race. Rather than resort to living life with what it offered her, instead she decided she was going to start fresh and new, and it paid off.

The plane touched down in Houston, Texas in December 1986. Another surprise awaited me: the airport was different from the one in Lagos—too many crowds came and went, the halls were larger and busier. At first, I considered myself lost. If not for the woman who helped me to contact my cousin who came to pick me up, I would have considered sleeping in the airport. Later, her son came to pick her up after she left me with $20 and a small note carrying details on how to reach her.

I felt an ugly air around me as I wove through the crowd, and when I was at customs, too many eyes were on me. I frowned at the thought of people looking at me like I was a terrorist. When my cousin arrived, he revealed that racism was the fence that separated blacks from whites over here.

Chapter Two
NOSTALGIC FLASHBACK

W hen I arrived in Houston, I saw it as a dream come true, and there were so many things to be excited about, but then, I remembered my family back at home. I was doing all of this for them.

Talking about family, I have a very good and strong one. We remained in the ways our mother had taught us and never for once drifted off course no matter the struggle we went through. When we were alone, my siblings and I learned to be strong on our own and not give up.

My name is Clifford Ubani, born in Ohanze Isiahia Aba, Abia State, Nigeria. I was born into this world around the late nineteen-fifties. I have two other siblings—an older brother and a younger sister. Our family was the typical hustling type where our parents worked hard to feed us. We were not rich, but we ate at least two full meals in a day.

At that time, I did not know much, but I understood pretty well that my family was not very okay and that our nation too was in a crisis, which was the civil war at that time—the war that claimed the life of my father, Mr. Ngwakwe William Ubani.

I was only ten at that time when death stepped on its cold feet into our home. When the news reached us, we were devastated. I remember how sad my mother's voice sounded when she wailed; in fact, it scared me more than the fact that our father was dead. She would scream in agony and then fall silent almost immediately. Many relatives came around, and it was then that I saw most of them for the first time. Neither my elder brother nor my sister cried, but I cried a lot. At night, I couldn't sleep despite the numerous calming assurances I got from every uncle and aunt. Was it possible for one not to mourn one's dead? Not that I felt anything sour when he died, but I cried because I saw it as a necessity. Three weeks after we received the news of his death, my father was buried, and my mother started the long and lonely journey of widowhood as custom demanded.

A week after my father was buried, we were thrown out of the house by my father's relatives. It was the beginning of my mother's travail. We were on our own now, and so the real hustle began in earnest—but first, my mother flung off the black attire which signified her mourning for her deceased husband. She got back on her feet when it was very clear that we wouldn't be getting any help from our father's relatives. My mother was a strong woman who would never give up. She had three kids to cater for on her own now, and so she went back fully into her petty business that had died down during the war. She contacted her customers to let them know she was back in business.

My mother, Mrs. Eliza Ubani Ngwakwe, began striving in earnest for my siblings and I to survive and also continue our education.

As one would expect from a typical Igbo woman, she took up other jobs in addition to her business, and when she came home at night, she was always tired. By now, I understood that we were struggling in our home and that my mother was also struggling hard for us. She'd always try to look strong for us, but I noticed her struggle anyway. It seemed like I was the one who understood it most, and so at eleven, my mind was fixed on doing something to help our family while my mother was away hustling. I was not the eldest—I had a big brother—but it seemed as if I was the one who reasoned most.

I started running errands for neighbors after school, for which I got a little change in return. I would fetch water into their large pots, clean their compounds or work on their farms. These people loved me a lot, they were intrigued by my unrelenting spirit, they had compassion for me, and so I got more money and material things. Of course, my mother was aware of my after-school work. She acted as if she was not pleased, but deep down inside, I could sense that she was really happy and full of gratitude. Eventually, she consented and encouraged me more. I started saving the money I was getting in an earthen box secretly locked away under my mother's bed.

Things continued for us that way, and we were used to it. In fact, it seemed to get better; my mother provided food and other necessary things while the money I saved was what my siblings and I used for school.

Life never stopped dealing with someone. I realized that when another tragedy hit our family four years after our father's death, the tragedy that shattered me completely. It was in 1972 when my mother passed away. I was fourteen then, so I was very aware of what was happening and what was at stake. At first, her death did not affect me as much as I had thought it would, and that was because for some reasons, it looked fictitious to me. I used to think she would wake up and show up right at the door, apologizing for sleeping so much and for scaring everyone, but at the same time, my mature gut told me she was dead, gone forever.

My mother had returned from work one day, and as usual, she was exhausted. Mother was always tired whenever she returned from the market, but she had the habit of keeping it from us. She never wanted us to see her weak side; she kept looking strong for us. I was the closest to her, and so I knew this weakness was not the usual type. The next day, she was ready for market, but we pleaded with her to rest for a day at least, and, well, she knew we were right.

Later in the day, things had gotten so much worse that she could barely talk. I was angry and sad because I knew something was wrong and yet I did not do anything. Some relatives came around and took her to the hospital. We had been administering the usual drugs she used whenever she was weak, but this was something worse. Mother had been living with typhoid fever. We got to know this at the hospital and also learned that it was too late because the illness had eaten deep due to negligence on her side. She died the following day.

For a week or two, some of our relatives came around consoling us in different ways. Some of them that were nice enough brought money while some thought it wise to bring material things. Later, everyone left us, and we were on our own. At first, we were not used to having to survive on our own, and so we would call our relatives with the hope of getting money from them or any form of help they could render, but we got nothing at all except excuses, and so we quickly adjusted to the new way of life. As soon as we ran out of money, I decided to go fully into the little jobs I'd been doing while my mother was still alive. I increased the number of houses I worked for, but I still managed to maintain my academics at the same time.

From a young age, even my primary school days, I was a bright kid. If I didn't come first, I'd come second, and the grades I had for each subject were always encouraging. This got me a lot of attention and sympathy from people, and as a result, my wages increased. There was this particular family I used to work for; they would feed me, give me fine clothes plus an extra tip added to my payment.

During this time, my younger sister attended school and did the work in our home while my brother and I worked for others. He mainly labored on people's farms. I remembered how we used to pray together at night after we have eaten dinner prepared by our sister, who was twelve at that time.

Thus the struggle continued till I completed my basic education. I had a few weeks of break before I sat for the Common Entrance Examination for secondary school. During these weeks, I had a lot of time, and so I worked in more homes in an attempt to save more money if I was going to further my education into the next level. Also, I knew I would have to leave home very soon as there was no secondary school in my village. Having saved enough, I obtained the form for the examination.

I wrote the exam, and when the results were released, I passed with flying colors. Also, I was offered admission into the only secondary school available in my vicinity and was scheduled to resume my education in two weeks. This was a very difficult thing for my siblings and I. We were all happy, but still, we wept. It was the first time we were going to be apart from each other. When the families I worked for heard I would be moving very soon, they were happy, but they were going to miss me. They gave me money and foodstuff.

Secondary school was a whole new world for me; everything was cumbersome and challenging. I knew I could not remain idle for too long and so I started looking for families that would let me work and live in their home and also pay me. Eventually, I got one, and they showed me lots of love, especially when they heard my story.

At first, striking a balance between schoolwork and housework was quite difficult. I had not gotten the hang of it and 'came to think it was an almost impossible task. I was keen to learn and be educated, but then, whenever the thought of quitting the after-school work so I could concentrate on my studies came to mind, I would shake it off. I knew I needed the money and all I needed to do was double up the time I spent on reading, so I did. Whenever I came back from school, the first thing I did was to go and pick up my boss' little girl from her school, then wash his car, feed the two big German shepherds in the house, and clean the compound if necessary.

As I mentioned, this family showed me love, the kind of love that I have not felt in a long time, and I in return never dared disappoint them. One of the things they did for me which I will be forever grateful for was grant the opportunity of going to see my family every Sunday.

My boss' wife would load me with lots of food and other material things whenever I went. This reduced the heavy burden on our heads a bit. My younger sister was still in elementary school while my big brother was a full-time farmer now; he worked on other people's farms during the week while he spent every weekend on his. Half of my monthly salary would be for my tuition, a quarter of the other half went into savings, and the rest I sent home.

We continued striving hard, hoping one day, things would get better, and it was getting better indeed: my grades in school had changed, and I was competitive for the top of the class. Some teachers had noticed me and called me countless times; some of them heard my story and encouraged me.

This way I continued till I was in my third year, when another setback came my way—the family I worked for were moving to the city. The news was good for them, but it struck me hard. Everything had started to blossom for me and all of a sudden, I could see it all going down the drain. My boss understood my worries, and he told me he would never forget me in as much as I was still in contact with me. They were angels to my siblings and I, and now they were leaving. I contacted my brother and sister and informed them about the latest development and of course, they were devastated too. At last, we came up with the idea of going to work for one of the teachers at the teachers' lodge till I found a new family that was willing to take me in. On the day my boss and his family were leaving, my siblings came around to bid them goodbye and thank them. They left us with money and other valuable things.

I needed a place to stay and work to get money to sponsor myself, so I went to one of our teachers who lived in the staff quarters. He took me in, and I in return would work for him. There was no payment involved, but I had no choice since a place to stay was a priority. Meanwhile, I had started looking for other families that were willing to have me in their house. During my stay in the staff quarters, I had enough time to work on my studies considering the little time I spent on chores.

I still visited my siblings every Sunday and gave them part of the little change I had. During this time, no relative checked up on us to see how we were doing, except my cousin, who was in the US. He was a year older and three classes ahead. I remembered how he'd share his plans with me to travel abroad after he completed his secondary school education. He eventually fulfilled those plans. Now he wrote to me twice a year.

After a time, I finally found a family who needed my service; it was for a short period, though, because they just had a baby and they needed someone to assist the madam of the house. The wage they offered was good, and it was the only offer I could get at that time, so I moved in with them. Working with the family was not as easy as I had pictured, although having to handle a whole house was not new to me, considering how I had helped my mother to take care of my younger sister. However, it affected my studies as I had little or no time for myself anymore.

Quitting was not an option for me; I just needed to double up the time I spent on reading and lessen the time I spent on resting. When I started working, I made the mistake of comparing the present family with the one I used to work for,, and it turned out to have a negative impact on my service to them. Luckily, I was quick to amend my ways. In all my time with this family, one of the good things that came my way was Ezinne, a girl I met at a party we attended at Ogbo Hill.

At the end of a year, my contract with the family came to an end, and as that time approached, I had gotten another family. As soon as I left the old family, I packed in with my new boss and his wife, with whom I stayed till it was time for me to sit for my Secondary School Certificate Examination (SSCE) in the year 1980. By then, I had saved enough money to obtain the form, but my boss insisted on paying for me. When the results were released, I passed as expected. I had A in mathematics, a B in English, a B in literature, an A in government and a C in Christian Religious Knowledge. My joy knew no bounds when I informed my siblings. I informed other people, like my former boss who had left for the city and my cousin in Houston. I tried writing to Ezinne, but she didn't get in touch even though we had written to each other a lot until we lost contact just before we started exams. To be honest, we were developing some kind of chemistry through letters even though we were miles apart; she remained one to be remembered.

I returned to my siblings, and the search for a new job started. When I first got back home, I began to work for three different families. I didn't sleep in their houses, though. My sister was in her first year in senior secondary school, and so we spared her the struggle so she would have all the time for her studies even though she protested, while my older brother and I did the whole thing. I had almost given up on the idea of searching for a better job, but then, there was a wild thought I secretly nursed in my mind: I wanted to travel abroad to father my education. Now, that was a big project, not obtaining an SSCE form. To travel out of Nigeria, I would need a lot of money. I continued searching for a better job, but the search didn't seem to be proving fruitful, and so I contacted my former boss in the city. It was through his help that I got the office of a clerk in the Nigerian Electric Power Authority (NEPA) in 1981, a year after I graduated from school.

Working at NEPA was stressful, but it was all fun to me. I couldn't have imagined myself working in such a big corporation. Due to the ever-burning passion I had for work and the big dream I intended to save for, I got the hang of the entire system in just a few weeks and I was very good: reliable, fast, and honest with my paperwork. This made my new boss love me. He saw me as a son and a younger brother, and so I revealed to him my plans to travel overseas and he encouraged me. I wrote to my cousin once in six months, telling him how well I was preparing.

When I was surely prepared to take the bold step, I contacted my cousin, finalized my plans, and I was ready. Of course, I had saved more than enough in all my years with NEPA. And so on December 20, 1986, I applied for study-leave, which I'm sure was received with mixed feelings, but my boss understood he had rendered help which would be forever remembered. With my plans concluded, after hugging my family for the umpteenth time, I left for Lagos.

Chapter Three
LIFE IN HOUSTON

Right from the airport, I had started receiving lots of amazing shocks which I couldn't believe because they were just too fantastic. I couldn't believe I was finally here, in Houston, thousands of miles away from my home. As we drove in my cousin's car, I hung out my head from the window like a spoilt dog enjoying the breeze in the back seat of a Jeep. Honestly, I had never seen a white man up close before except in the papers; they were more real than the ones in the book, just like the way the world outside the plane window had resembled, yet exceeded the old globe on my headmaster's table back in my elementary school. I looked on as grown women attached short ropes to the necks of dogs which they walked with by the roadside.

In short, everything surprised me, including the cold. I had missed that particular detail in my cousin's letter, and unfortunately for me, I arrived at the coldest time of the year, but I was too excited to mind that. I blinked, and a tear rolled down my cheek. I wished my mother was alive to see her son in a place like this, to see that her son was in the white man's land. I thought about my older brother and younger sister too, and I promised myself that I would never fail them.

I arrived Houston, Texas in December 1986, happy and full of hot blood, waiting to see what the city had in store for me. Initially, my goal was to further my education. A million questions rumbled in my head, and I was scared that my cousin would eventually get tired of having to listen to my blabbing, but what could I do? I was still surprised by how someone would lead a huge dog with a small rope.

My attention was drawn to the number of black people I noticed on the street that we turned to now. Most didn't look like Nigerians or people from any other African country for that matter, but their skin was black, just like mine. Some of them braided their hair, and so I concluded they must have been here for a long time considering how a man would have a hair that long unless he were an *oyinbo* person.

We negotiated a left bend and then another one. Next we took a right turn and then another right. We took lots of rights. I couldn't keep the excitement all to myself anymore, and so I asked my first question, "Did the dogs we saw earlier steal meat from their owners' pots?"

Honestly, I had never seen such a puzzling sight as this one before, even though I once took care of dogs when I worked as a house helper. My cousin threw me a quizzical look, one hand on the steering wheel and the other on his lap. He laughed hard before tapping me on the shoulder.

"They did not steal any meat from the pot, Clifford. They are pets, and their owner is taking them for a walk. And it's called a leash, not rope," he explained, still laughing.

"Oh..." I cooed and shifted my gaze back to the roadside, watching as many things drifted past us.

I spoke again. "Why are we taking so many rights? Their road here is not straight." This time, my cousin did not reply; he just smiled and continued taking rights. After some time, he turned a little button on the dashboard and a song I couldn't make out the lyrics to started booming from every angle inside the car.

"Is this a church song?" I asked, pointing to the radio.

"Why?" my cousin asked. Obviously, he had gotten the iota of foolishness in my question.

"I mean, it sounds like they are speaking in tongues, like it's a Holy Ghost convention like we have during..."

My cousin busted into a long and hard laugh, cutting me short in my nonsense sentence.

"Damn!" my cousin said amidst laughter. "Clifford, they are called rappers, and they are rapping right now, that's why you can't hear them quite well."

I continued asking questions, not minding the shunning answers I kept getting in return. Who wouldn't have questions to ask? We had taken lots of turns now, and it looked like we were traveling. My mouth had refused to run, and so I decided to give myself some rest. Later, after taking another turn, he told me the next street was where we lived. I eased back into my seat with happiness after the announcement, but then the car stopped—there was some kind of crowd in the middle of the road. My cousin killed the engine and hopped out of the car after giving me stern and specific warnings not to come out, and I obeyed. I watched as he disappeared into the crowd.

Apparently, there had been a fight between a white cop and a black driver. The cop had pulled the black driver over and later charged him with some kind of offense—which the accused had quickly debunked, but the cop was not ready to listen, and in no time, a simple argument had escalated into a big fight, leaving the driver in a bad state. No one offered to help him, not even blacks like him! They all just went about their business, leaving the wounded man in the middle of the road, sprawling in pain. It was exactly like the story we were told in Sunday school. The story of the good Samaritan who helped someone who was attacked by thieves.

I could see the anger on my cousin's face as we drove on in silence until we arrived at his house—a big building with three bedrooms and a large sitting room. There, I got another shock from the materials in the room. Immediately upon entering the house, my cousin had disappeared into one of the rooms, leaving me to feel at home, and that was exactly what I did. I felt around the entire sitting room with my hands, carefully caressing things. I would lift things, twirl them gingerly in my hand, and then return them to their positions, exactly the way I met them. When I was sure I had fed my curious and surprised eyes enough, I fell back into a sofa positioned next to the door. I felt the softness and couldn't ask for anything better; it was way better than the ones in my boss's sitting room back in my village, even though they seemed like the best at that time. I stood up and walked to the window, where I saw grown men in armless clothes walking on the street in groups. There was a sound of old music playing somewhere, and also the clumsy sound of barking dogs.

I was still lost in the world of Houston when my cousin came into the large room. He was not smiling. *Is he still angry from the incident earlier?* I thought as I quickly returned to my seat like a small boy who wouldn't want to annoy his father lest he be denied the chance of going to the city. In my case, I didn't want my cousin to send me back to Abia State, Nigeria. I took a long, good look at my cousin and I couldn't help but wonder at how neat and nourished he looked, even though I had looked chubbier whenever we compared sizes when he was still in Nigeria. No doubt this place must have some kind of ointment that nourished people's skin.

Finally, my cousin cleared his throat and spoke.

"Clifford, you're no longer in Nigeria where everything happens the way you want. This is Houston."

I nodded twice, knowing he still had more to say.

"What you saw earlier is the reality around here. Even with the law as strong or capable as they may have painted it, it still has no regard for blacks." He rubbed his neat hair and looked me squarely in the eye. "The same thing happened at the airport. These white people don't like you; they hate you, Clifford. They hated you the moment you set foot into their country."

I tried bending my neck to nod, but it wouldn't move. The impact of those words burdened my young neck, silencing every excitement I have been enjoying the whole day. The words sank deep into my heart, waking up the guard in me. My cousin noticed the change on my face and quickly said something to calm my nerves.

"Don't be scared, bro, you won't be a victim as long as you play by the rules."

Later that night, he made dinner, and after we ate, we talked a lot about many things. We talked about the first time he arrived here, we talked about the mistakes he made, the fights he got into and the rules he broke, and lastly, we talked about his upcoming marriage to a Yoruba girl he met some years back in Houston before we decided to call it a day. He showed me my room and promising that we would do the real talking the next day.

The first thing I did was wash myself in the warm shower before jumping into bed. I thought about my parents, especially my mum. We used to talk about going to the white man's country to learn and here I was now, to learn in the white man's country, but she wasn't there to celebrate with me. I thought about my father too, how happy he would be when he had boasted about me in front of his friends. My mind wandered over to my siblings, wondering what they were doing currently. I thought about Ezinne too. Lastly, I said a great deal of prayer, which consisted of thanksgiving mostly, before I finally drifted off to sleep.

The following day, I woke up late, later than the time I was used to back at home. At first, I thought I did not see clearly, but when I squinted my eyes and peered closely at the little clock sitting on a small stool beside my bed, I saw that the time was 7:00 AM. I sprang up from the soft bed like a rabbit that manages to wriggle itself free from a snare. Normally, I woke up at 5:00 AM, but today was an exception. Well, what did I expect after a thirteen-hour journey? I dragged myself out of bed into the bathroom, and as directed by my cousin, I used every piece of equipment properly. In no time, I was in the sitting room, where I met my cousin, and judging by the aroma that greeted me, I knew he had made breakfast.

While we ate, he started telling me about everything I should know about my new environment. He told me about this neighborhood: who to avoid, who to befriend, who to greet from afar and who not to greet at all. As he talked, I listened with rapt attention, noting every detail in my mind. He warned me about girls, but I quickly told him I was not into them and besides, I would be leaving the area for college very soon. He warned me about the cops, too. He emphasized the fact that they hated it when a black argued with them or tried to challenge them, but assured me that I wouldn't be having any trouble if I didn't break any rule.

The conversation drifted into another new topic—the main reason why I came here. Actually, I had expected him to make plans prior to my arrival, but he didn't do much; he wanted me to be around in person first before he took any step. He listed out the names of different colleges and their requirements and cost. Eventually, we decided that Houston Community College was the best option for me, and so the conversation led to the most important aspect, which is money. I revealed to my cousin that I didn't have more than $200 on me, plus the $20 the madam I met at the Lagos airport gave me when we touch down at Houston. This led to the conclusion that I needed to work so I could save money if I were ever going to consider processing any admission into any college.

As we discussed further, my mind went back to the gruesome event that we witnessed yesterday. My cousin laughed when I brought it up.

"Look, Clifford, racism has been an ancient plague here, and you just can't expect it to go away like that. It's in the system here in the US, and we are in the US. It's a war, Clifford, a lost one. It's no longer about winning; it's all about survival now."

His words cut deep into my innocent heart; I thought I was going to cry. Why did it have to be that way? Had the ancient blacks before us committed a particular crime that caused this? I remembered the cop and the driver again, and I couldn't help but imagine if it was me in that kind of situation. Would I have been helpless like the black driver? Or would I have run to the law for help? This development was new to me, and I started seeing it as darkness clouding over me.

Later, when my cousin was leaving for work, he offered a ride if I would love to go with him. I jumped at the offer and so an hour later, we arrived at the bakery where he worked. It was an opportunity for me to see more of Houston and also meet new people. I got to meet my cousin's friends—some of whom were whites, but mostly, his closest friends were black. They loved my inquisitive habit, and so I made friends too. In fact, I met one of them, a Nigerian, and he was from my state. Honestly, he was happy to see me, and before long, he was bombarding me with thousands of questions to which I gave satisfactory answers.

On our way back home later in the day, my cousin announced that he had found a job for me at a cafeteria.

It was a surprise to me when my cousin broke the news that I would resume work in two day's time, but I was really happy. He taught me some keywords and other things that would help me during my service. I started working at the cafeteria the following week. During my longest shift, I worked six hours a day, and I worked five hours during my short shifts. I was saving money, but I knew it wouldn't be enough when I eventually gained admission to the college. I figured I would need to work elsewhere during my off hours, but I had already applied for admission. Also, I didn't want to overload my day yet. I talked to my cousin, and we agreed to calm down till I got admitted first. Then I would calculate the hours I'd be spending on classes every day and the spare hours I'd have left; this was to know the type of job I'd opt for.

I wrote to my siblings when I got the job, telling them all about my trip to Houston. I remembered to mention the old lady I met at the airport, too. I shared with them my experience since I had arrived in Houston. I told them about my job, the friends I'd made, and also, I mentioned the neighborhood we lived in. I wanted to write many things, but I didn't get the chance, yet I still managed to tell them every important detail they would love to hear.

Two weeks later, I received a piece of mail one morning carrying the news that I had been admitted into Houston Community College to study criminal justice. I had been pretty sure I would be admitted, but still, the news came as a surprise. My joy knew no bounds as I danced around the house. I called the old lady, and she was very happy for me; in fact, she sent me $100 and promised to help in any way she could. I was getting close to achieving my dreams, and all I needed to do was to be focused. I remembered my parents, and I was not sad this time. Rather, I was happy and grateful.

Chapter Four
LIFE IN COLLEGE

T he first day in school couldn't be termed the best for me—
it usually isn't the best for anyone, but mine seemed like
the worst of them all. I was not used to changing schools
or having to go through the trouble of getting used to the environments of a new school, considering the state of things back at my
village. There was only one school for everyone, and you would have
to graduate from the particular school where you started your education. We didn't have many schools, so no one changed schools. But
as an enthusiastic young man, I was determined to learn so badly
that I made sure petty limitations never affected or distracted me. I
had no difficulty blending in with my new environment, and it was
then that I realized that I was in a different world that had the same
compatible rotten vice.

I noticed the darkness in the school was not like the one I've
seen outside. The one I saw here was the typical kind of bad attitude

associated with teens and young adults. Finally, I concluded that the virus had eaten deep into the roots of the system that oversaw everything. It saddened me more that the school authority couldn't even do anything about it--it was exactly like the one happening on the outside, where the law couldn't curb racism but claimed to have eradicated it totally. It was the part where the government of this country had failed most. I was sure there were students that are innocent and not corrupted from their home, but they were caught in the snare already laid down for any careless game to hop in blindly.

The college was a green field where every bird could fly to any direction it pleased. The school that was supposed to be the ultimate home of learning was now a place where students felt free to come and hide or escape the grip of their parents. The outcome was that any student who was bad from home would get worse once they were in college. There were many unimaginable errors in the system which would need more than just adjustment. I was young too, just like most of them, but I was seeing with African eyes; I hated their lifestyles. I was shocked when I saw things that we would normally consider taboo in Nigeria being treated as things of little significance to the perpetrators.

Despite these things, I never looked to my right or left. I was too focused to be distracted. Occasionally, when I felt oppressed or depressed, I would remember my mother's words about success on the finish line waiting for whoever endured the race unto the end. I kept my head low and went about my business, trying as much as possible to avoid any unnecessary attention, and if I ever found myself in such a situation, I had ways of wriggling myself out. I rarely spoke to anyone, nor did I join any group or club of any kind—not that I didn't approve of socialization, but I just wanted to concentrate on my studies without being noticed by anyone. I observed as much as I could for two weeks. During this time I spent most of my breaks in the library, all in a bid to avoid every possible trouble. I stayed in my lane with my head low.

Finally, after I had watched and learned enough, I decided to make friends. My community back home had turned me into some kind of a paranoid person, but of course, it was all thanks to my upbringing. Knowing full well the impact that friends have on one's life, I took my time, and at last, I associated myself with three blacks: a Nigerian, a Kenyan, and a black American. I had a lot in common with these people; we shared the same views about life generally. We did almost everything together: we studied together, walked together, and sat together, but still we maintained a low profile.

My friends and I worked together on projects and assignments. We had different rooms in college, but still, we found a way to be together. Luckily, we all had the habit of reading; we were bookworms. Also, all three of us had jobs after school hours. I retained my job at the cafeteria. Initially, when I gained admission into college, I told my employer, Mrs. Brown, and she agreed to let someone take over when I was away. Balancing my job with schoolwork was quite easy for me, but I knew I would need another job very soon when I considered how my expenses were feeding fat on my savings.

I informed Mrs. Brown about my plan to quit, and she understood even though it was with a heavy heart that she let me go. I realized how much my services meant to her, but I had to enlarge my coast if I was going to see myself through college.

I heard about a vacancy at a factory, and after making inquiries, I was delighted to hear that the hours wouldn't interfere with my schoolwork, and so I took the job. The factory paid me quite well, but it was not enough, so I took up another job as a delivery boy. At times, everything would seem almost too difficult for me, but I was strong-willed. I focused on the prize at the end of the race. The two jobs were only on weekdays, and so I was always free during weekends, which I didn't like, so I opted for a third job at a laundry shop. Now I had three stressful jobs to work and loads of books to read, plus a compilation of assignments to complete and submit.

One could classify my first year as the same as my first day at college. That first year came and went, but not with its lessons. Sadly, learning after failing was not the ideal way of learning. Academically, I didn't excel quite as well as I had expected. I missed out on a few things at the beginning. When I told my cousin about my results, he told me not to beat myself up. I still had time to make up for whatever mistake I might have made. Also, he said mistakes should be the foundation on which new attempts are built.

I braced myself up, encouraging myself with the fact that I was still new to the system and that I was competing with rich kids who didn't have to work three jobs after school instead of reading their books, that I was competing with students who didn't have to worry about sponsoring themselves through college, that I was competing against kids who had been in the system long before I started nursing the dream of traveling abroad.

By the end of the second year, I had gotten used to the system, and my grades were far better than my first year's. I had learned everything there is to learn about college and what it offers, and from my mistakes in the past, I bucked up and started afresh. I had learned how to use technology, and I was able to do research on my own. This helped and boosted my capability to learn very quickly. However, regardless of the vicinity or the area, blacks always topped every position, as far as I'd seen in my years in Houston. In my class, for instance, two blacks were among the first three students. In other areas like sport, music, and even competitions, blacks were always there to lead.

During my second year, I found myself in situations that could have put my whole existence as far as Houston was concerned in jeopardy. A third-year student had crossed my path twice, accusing me of having a secret relationship with his girlfriend, who was just a friend to me and nothing more. I didn't owe this guy any explanation—I was way older than he was, but my age was just a number here, what mattered was that a black man had snatched a white man's girlfriend. I knew I could have just taught him a lesson like I would do with my younger siblings back in Nigeria but I didn't have that kind of power. So whenever he approached me, I'd keep mute and he, in turn, would rant on and leave when he realized I wouldn't budge.

One day, he came at me as usual, but this time, he came to apologize. I was angry, yet surprised. I could sense the genuineness in his voice as he pleaded. I calmed down and pulled him into my arms. I got to know that his girlfriend actually told him the whole truth. A new friendship sprouted between Kelvin and I, even though some blacks were not happy with what I did—they had expected me to beat some sense into his head or keep him quiet in an aggressive way. There were some who even offered to deal with him on my behalf, in fact. A black student advised me to sleep with the s girl and make a video of the sight-souring act for him to see, but I shunned them all; the words my cousin spoke to me when I first arrived never left my heart.

The third year came with its own challenges, different from the ones of the previous years. My schoolwork increased and got harder. In fact, I thought of dropping one of the three jobs, but I remembered I had bills to pay and myself to sponsor, so all I did was to triple my effort. My cousin's wedding was fast approaching. It would be the same time as my graduation—how time flies! My cousin was the only relative who decided to check on my siblings and I after we lost our parents; he was a nice guy who I would forever be indebted to.

I was still in the third year of school when Kelvin graduated. He had requested my presence and also assigned tasks to me regarding the family party he planned to hold at his house later in the day. I supplied the DJ and made the decorations, too. He was indeed a friend I never regretted having. He taught me a lot of things about college life and beyond. He was like a sibling to me, and speaking of siblings, my elder one wrote to me at that time, detailing the recent happenings. It was in the letter that I learned they had moved to the city and that my brother now had a job, while that my sister was in her final year in secondary school. My heart warmed up, and I almost cried for these positive developments.

I applied myself to my final exams and, taking a glance at my records, one would say I did a good job; in fact, I finished among the top ten in my class. I was not expecting anything less, considering how much I had prepared and my previous results, yet I was still surprised. Graduating with excellent grades against all the odds was not a small thing. My cousin had a small party for me, inviting every person in the neighborhood. I wrote to my siblings too, and from their reply, they were very happy for me. I called the old woman, and she was happy too; she gave me money. I also wrote to my boss at NEPA, where I used to work back in my village.

I became a graduate, having earned myself an Associate's Degree in Criminal Justice in the year 1991. Now, everyone expected that I was going to go into the workforce fully and make more money and probably settle down with a wife. Well, I wanted to settle down with a beautiful lady and have kids and a good job, but I wanted more. I wanted to read more, and so I applied for a Bachelor's Degree in Criminal Justice at the University of Houston-Downtown. Some of my friends had resisted the idea, but I was determined, and nothing could discourage me when I'd fixed my mind on something. Eventually, I was admitted into the university, and so I moved out of my cousin's house and opted for accommodation close to the university campus; I changed my job for a better one, too.

Chapter Five
NO LIMITATIONS
FOR PASSION

∽∾∾∾

Five years in Houston and I was no longer the newbie from Nigeria. I was now the black boy from Nigeria in the US with a Western certificate, about to get a second degree. University was nothing like I had imagined; at first, I had lots of challenges, but because of my foundation from Nigeria, I was quick to adapt and came through stronger than ever. My hustle became harder, but I did what I always do: triple my effort. In Nigeria, after Western education was accepted, and the people saw the improvement it brought to the land, everyone capable wanted their children to learn to read and write, and it was this perspective that drove me to want to learn more, that made me think if I didn't read enough, I wouldn't be accepted. University life had its juicy parts, but I rarely had time to enjoy it because I was always busy.

During my first year, I saw many things that baffled me. They were greater versions of the things I observed in the college. During my first week back at school, two senior students were expelled on drug charges. I was shocked; I had seen things like that back in my cousin's neighborhood, but never had I expected to find it in the university. So, once I had seen the vice dominating the university, I was quick to make a stand for myself. As my mother used to say, "If you don't stand for anything, you will fall for everything." This saying helped me a lot when I was asked to join fraternities or any form of a gang. My answer was always "NO."

I devoted my time to studying and work. This made people love me and even used me as an example to preach for their own folks.

I was young and hardworking, and as a law student, I was aware of the dangers of being caught in some kind of unholy gathering by the law. I was black with no one at the top, so I was condemned automatically. A second consideration was the certificate I was yearning and working hard to get; it would all be forfeited. Also, I would be a shame to my family, and I was not willing to risk all that for some unreasonable thing.

In all these scary milestones, learning in the university still had its fun. Maybe it was just me who always loved learning or it was just passion. In fact, it was a passion for bringing true justice to life that pushed me into studying criminal justice. By now, I had seen how rotten the system had gotten, and it wouldn't heal itself unless someone stood up for the task. My cousin once told me that racism was in America's DNA and so ending racism would mean turning over America totally, turning the whole of America upside down and burn out every last bit of injustice, but who would do that?

For all these scary experiences, learning in the university still had its fun. Maybe it was just that I always loved learning, or else it was passion. In fact, it was a passion for bringing true justice to life that pushed me into studying criminal justice. By now, I had seen how rotten the system had gotten, and it wouldn't heal itself unless someone stood up to do the task. My cousin once told me that racism was in America's DNA and so ending racism would mean turning over America totally, turning the whole of America upside down and burning out every last bit of injustice, but who would do that?

I nursed the dream of becoming an officer of the law, but it was never going to happen if I was behind bars or if I had tarnished my records by mingling with the wrong company, and so I kept in my lane. I put my time and resources into community services, attended countless public hearings, and also discussed legal topics with lots of legal practitioners and active officers. My project was a cumbersome one, but I delivered on it anyway with the help of people I conversed with at the Department of Criminal Justice (DCJ). I focused my research on the connection between small crimes and large-scale crimes like bank robbery and serial murders, and I was able to establish the fact that neither could one work without the other. Both are equations that needed to be solved simultaneously.

I finished my university education in 1994 and graduated with a Bachelor of Science in Criminal Justice from the University of Houston- Downtown. I was sufficient enough now that I was able to send money to my siblings in Nigeria. I had cultivated the habit of writing to my family after every breakthrough, and this time when I wrote to them, they expressed their longing to see me back home, but I was not done with learning yet. I had applied for a graduate program in public administration at Texas Southern University (TSU), and I received an offer of admission. After having accumulated fifteen credits, I dropped out of the TSU without completing the program.

After quitting the TSU, I went for a Criminal Justice Program that taught me everything about being a police officer.

There, I learned the arts and acts of investigating cases. I learned the unique step-by-step skills that shouldn't be ignored when conducting any investigation or carrying out an interrogation. I was taught how to follow a lead and how to handle evidence at crime scenes and during transportation. I also learned how to handle witnesses. One of the things the police department valued so much was evidence and witness testimony; in fact, if a witness or evidence was compromised by an officer, he might lose his job. The trainings were not easy, but I loved them, and I assimilated very quickly.

As our graduation neared, we were allowed to tag along with experienced officers for the real field work, to put into practice everything we have learned. Once I was a tagalong with an officer, and he assigned me the task of interrogating a witness of rape. As I walked into the dark, silent room, fear gripped me. I knew all these things, I knew what to say, I knew where to start, but for a reason, I was just not able to speak. However, after some time, I braced myself and began to interrogate the witness, and eventually, I was able to successfully draw out valuable information that helped us to catch the rapist and also solve the case. In the end, I was congratulated and rewarded.

At times, I find it funny when I realize the obvious fact that I was training to be an enforcer of the law I once detested so much, but it was the opportunity I felt I would need if I were going to make an impact. After all, it was from the inside that the law needed repairing, and so it would be done by someone from the inside. To be honest, I saw another side of the law as I studied it more. I got to know why the officers did what they did and how and why the law worked the way it did. Only people who had the chance to study the law would understand it. This didn't justify the fact that it was biased, but it was not as spoilt as I as an outsider used to think. I promised myself that I would work hard and make a difference one way or the other.

It was during the program that I was taught how to use a variety of weapons; I was trained in every form of combat, too. This was the most stressful part of my training, but it was the one I loved the most. Back in Nigeria when I had the chance of seeing movies in a local cinema, I remember fantasizing about carrying out a weapon and shooting brown bad guys or flexing my muscles and, well, here I was now, actually training to be the commando I used to dream about as a kid. I was trained to disable potentially armed suspects, to chase down a running suspect to pick door locks in case of emergencies, and different tricks and tactics that could save lives. Truth be told, it was fun.

The most crucial training I had was learning to penetrate to, interact with, disable, disarm, save, or attack someone psychologically. This part was tedious; in short, it was the part where we had to learn how to deal with different types of people on different grounds with different conditions. I learned how to deal with problems, how to interact with people, how to calm them to be able to withdraw information from them. I learned to understand them. This meant I had to know the motive behind their actions, considering how people could burst and do big, bad, unreasonable things for no reason. Certainly, they are not in their right mind, but that doesn't allow them to hurt innocent people. Still, they are citizens of the US, and they have rights too, rights that must be respected all times no matter what.

I came to the realization that every level has a different devil. That is, every step on my journey since I lost my parents had involved different challenges, but despite all odds, I was able to break through every wall: having to sponsor my siblings and myself through elementary school with money I got from families I worked for till I got to secondary school, where I did the same thing until I graduated, then working at NEPA and then traveling to the US, and finally surviving through college with three jobs to work and then university also. In short, I had come a long way and I was still running.

Chapter Six
REWARD FOR
HARD WORK

ith a week to the completion of the program, I had successfully secured employment in Harris County Community Supervision as a probation officer. I was happy to take the job and couldn't wait for the program to end. I had high hopes. I'd always wanted to be involved in something like it, to help people lead a better life. My job ranged from managing the records of the parolee to intervention and supervision, managing cases, being part of court proceedings and conducting general assessments of parolees.

My first job, once a case was referred to me, was to carry out an assessment on the offender. I would contact the offender and his or her family and also reach out to the law enforcement personnel in charge of the case. I would join the relevant authorities to gather information about the offender's health and lifestyle. It was also my job to use the information gathered during the assessment to formulate and document strategies that would help the parolee get better and lead a better life. Additionally, I provided support during court proceedings. I would accompany the parolee to the court and provide support for organizational recommendations for the parolee.

A particular case was assigned to me: a thirty-two-year-old male citizen who was sentenced to jail for thirteen years for raping a minor. I worked hand in hand with relevant personnel along with the parolee to help him get back on his feet. His records showed that he had been charged to court on several occasion for abuse. I recommended that he be placed in a rehabilitation program after finding out from his medical records that he had a behavioral disorder. The man was placed on a daily treatment, and within six months, he showed great signs of improvement. I handled another case within the same period; this time the young parolee was in for drug and substance abuse. He was also placed in rehab.

Both parolees, within one year, came clean.

There were other cases that involved mental disorders and something traceable to family history. Handling such persons was not entirely easy, but it was a job a deliberately signed up for, and as such, I didn't have any excuse to give. Plus, I loved the job. Whenever I was given a case, the first thing I did was to check the person's criminal record and health record; then, I would look at the crime and see if there was a victim. If there was, I would get the necessary permissions to initiate contact with the victim and the victim's family to gather more information. I had tremendous success as a probation officer with the Harris County Community Supervision and Corrections Department.

My boss loved me and the way I handled each case. He once told me he wished he had more officers like me. We laughed it off that day and continued with what we were doing. The only problem I had was the fact that I was a black man. I got praise, but others got the raise and the promotion.

I was very professional with each case and tried not to be emotional. It was part of the training we received not to let our personal feelings interfere with a case. It was okay to feel a certain way, but never okay to act based on how we felt. At all points, our goal was to put lives and the law first.

There were times when we found ourselves at cross roads. In such situations we were allowed to act in ways that did not obstruct justice and at the same time did not endanger parolees. Of course, we knew the consequences of taking laws into our hands; it has led a lot of good officers into prison and caused some of them to be dismissed from the police force. For every officer, dismissal for rash decisions and mistakes was considered an embarrassment and shameful way of losing your job. It was worse when you end up behind bars. Hard choices were made at different times, but I was always careful never to let my decisions become a reason I lost my job.

Every difficult case we cracked attracted a bonus for me. There were times when I helped establish a link between a small crime and something bigger. That was thanks to my project during my bachelor's degree program. I used most of the findings I made then to solve a lot of puzzles. They helped me narrow down problems and even allowed me to ask the relevant questions, connecting all the dots more easily than a lot of my colleagues ever did. When cases became difficult, I was always asked to help out. Teamwork was one thing I enjoyed. As much as I achieved success working alone, my greatest success always came when I worked with people. I had a good record with teamwork, too. Most times, I just listened and did less talking. Sometimes, I was the one doing most of the talking.

My Nigerian background and how I lived through school allowed me to pay attention to details. I never left any stone unturned. My colleagues sometimes would say that I had the perfectionist syndrome, that I always wanted things done perfectly. Yes, they were right. I was the type of officer who would consider all the options I had before choosing a particular option to work with. I was never known to give up. When things didn't work out with a particular option, I didn't just opt for the alternative; I would go back and re-evaluate the entire process. Perhaps we were missing out on some details that were relevant to our course.

That perfectionist syndrome was something I inherited from my late mother. It followed me from home, and it helped me a lot. However, there were times when it delayed the process and almost got me into trouble with some of my colleagues and with some families. Somehow, I always managed to avert the problems. I knew when I was too careful and when I needed to discontinue on a path.

After two years of work, I decided to change the category of people I would be dealing with. I cross-trained as a juvenile probation officer with the Serious Offender Supervision Division. It was a state grant program. I loved the job so much as I was exposed to a much younger set of offenders. I got the chance to interact with young adults with serious criminal records. For some of them, I felt enormous pity, while some were directly responsible for their predicaments. Some of the adolescents grew up with a single parent who barely had time for them; they had to work out certain things on their own. They got the wrong advice and ended up making the bad decisions that landed them in juvenile prisons.

Some of them grew up under the roof of parents who have been arrested several times for one criminal offense or the other. Such kids had a lot of difficulty becoming who they wanted to be. Listening to these kids sometimes made me so emotional. I imagined what life was like for them. I could relate with a lot of their stories because I was almost raised by a parent, except I lost mine before I knew my right from wrong. My story was harder than a lot of theirs, but we had different environments and what was permitted in Nigeria was not allowed in the US.

I shared my story with some of them and used it to encourage them. For some, it worked, while others just said I was lucky. I hated it when they tried to make excuses for their failures. At their ages I was already taking care of other mouths, something none of them would have been able to do.

During my time as a Juvenile Probation Officer, I had two very interesting cases that filled me with much surprise. The first was a young girl whose eighteenth birthday was three months away at the time her case was brought to us. When my boss instructed that I supervise her, she was pregnant. It wasn't the pregnancy before she was eighteen that shocked me; teenage pregnancy was a common story in the US. I was surprised that she was pregnant with her fifth child. As her supervisor, I went through her records and found that she had all five babies from different fathers. I was shocked to learn that. But just when I thought I was done getting surprising information about her, her records showed that she actually started getting pregnant at the age of twelve.

That was something that took me quite some time to absorb. I tried to imagine how a twelve-year-old girl could successfully carry a child and have a safe delivery. Apparently, she was one of those girls who experienced early puberty, and she also got wrong information and ended up confiding in the wrong people. She had little or no knowledge about menstruation, and when she experienced hers, she went to the wrong person for advice because her parents didn't have time for her. She was one of those kids from a broken home. It was common in the US to have kids from broken homes turn out like that. Some had voids in them that their single parents couldn't fill and so they developed habits that caused them more burdens than they could carry.

The girl in question had her first child at age twelve and at the age of fourteen she had another. As she turned fifteen, she was already pregnant with a third child, at seventeen she had her fourth, and just before she turned eighteen, she was pregnant with her fifth child. We had to subject her to a lot of treatments, considering the time she first became pregnant and the intervals between each birth. It was too much for a girl her age and something that might leave her permanently damaged. I helped her through the process of her healing, and she actually got better emotionally and mentally. That was the first time I saw such a situation—I only heard of others.

The second case was that of a rape. In my years of working, I've come across lots of such cases, but this one was different; it was nothing like I've heard or seen before. It was two months after the case of the pregnant eighteen-year-old was referred to us. The offender here was a thirteen-year old-boy who lost his single mother earlier that year, and so the authorities decide to make his sister his legal guardian. At that time she already had four kids. The boy moved into his sister's house and began to rape his two-year-old niece. The abuse continued until the little girl was infected, and she was taken to a hospital where she later died. Later, I learned that she was raped by her uncle several times.

The boy was accused and tried as an adult, and after being found guilty by the judge, he was sent to jail with a sentence of life imprisonment. His case made people cry but the law didn't work. Of course, there were other cases too, but these two were the ones that got to me the most.

Chapter Seven
LOVE AT LAST

It was on a Monday morning when a young boy was brought to our station. Apparently, he had been involved in a gunfight with a rival gang which left lots of bullets in his body.

Immediately, we wheeled him into an available car and rushed him to the hospital. We would have been delayed if we had not provided our badge, but he was moved into the operating theatre at once while we waited outside anxiously. I was with two other officers. Some nurses with different items in their hands started trooping into the theatre. It was then that I noticed one of them who looked like someone I knew. I was not sure yet and I couldn't call out due to the urgent business going on at that time, so I decided to wait till everything was calm. My attention was divided now; a part of me was thinking about the poor kid fighting for his life and another was focused on the person I thought I used to know.

Exactly thirty minutes later, the doors to the operating room opened and a young doctor walked out. He came to us and updated us about the condition of the boy, after which we signed different documents and the patient was transferred into the ward. While we remained with the doctor, the nurses started coming out, and I saw her. I was still not sure yet, but I had to try, so I turned away from the doctor and called, "Ezinne!"

I almost jumped out of my skin when she turned back.

"Ezinne!" I called again, but by this time I had started walking toward her already. As I approached her, I could tell she was surprised too. She began to walk toward with me with a disturbed look on her face. When we stood facing each other, I could see her eyes scanning my face, and suddenly, she called my name, "Clifford!"

I smiled and pulled her into my arms. We remained that way for some time until I remembered we were in the hospital, her place of work. We didn't have much time to talk, so we agreed to meet after work and catch up over dinner.

The talk we had that night opened the door to reviving the connection we used to have back in the village. She told me all that had happened after we lost contact, how she got here and became a registered nurse at the hospital where we met earlier in the day.

We started dating, and after six months, I proposed to her, and she said yes. We got married two months later. It was the beginning of my family life. We had four kids: two boys and two girls, plus a girl I had from my first girlfriend in Houston, Texas. Whenever I remembered how I had met the love of my life, I would acknowledge that God allowed everything that happened to me to happen and it was for a reason.

Our kids were good and honest children. They were loved by everyone in our neighborhood because of their good character. Looking at them makes me feel that I'm just lucky to have kids who turned out to be responsible. Well, I made sure that they were brought up in the Nigerian way; there were rules and regulations. I made sure they believed in and feared God, too. People who knew me very well would say they took after me, which I didn't doubt considering how they developed a passion for learning at the age of six. By that early age, each of them had already made a choice of what they wanted to study in the university. We encouraged them all along and gave them the support they needed. They were always among the best in their classes. They would run home to tell my wife and me how they were honored in school. Each of them knew how to make us happy. We loved them so much and were willing to do anything to make them happy.

My children grew up to become successful, and for that, I am very thankful to God. Despite everything we went through together and what they went through on their own, they still came out very well. My first child took the path of her mother and graduated with a Bachelor's of Nursing degree (BSN). It was a cause of joy at home. She went further to pursue an advanced degree in nursing. The second girl completed a B.Sc. in Biology and went ahead to pursue a career in pharmacy. She will be graduating in May 2019 with a Doctor of Pharmacy Degree. Our third daughter is a nineteen-year-old first-year student at the university. Our first boy graduated in May 2018 with Doctor of Pharmacy degree. He sat for his Board of Pharmacy Exam and passed very well and now works in the University of Texas Galveston facility. Meanwhile, our second boy graduated with BS, Electrical Engineering on December 14, 2018, and already had a job offer with USAA. These feats are worth rejoicing at, but unfortunately, their parents won't be around to witness it.

Chapter Eight
THE ENTREPRENEUR

A few years after marriage, I quit my position as a juvenile probation officer. As much as I loved and had passion for the job, I wanted to put my entrepreneur mind to work. It was a big risk, but one that I was willing to take, and so after I was sure of what I wanted, I discussed it with my wife and she reasoned and agreed with me. I also sought the help of people who had been in the system before me for every bit of advice I would need. When I was sure and set, I opened a storefront.

I got the idea of selling home appliances, and after doing thorough research about the market, the people I would be competing with, and everything else I needed to know, I stocked my store. The first year was neither good or bad; it was so-so.

I already knew what to expect in the first year of any business, and so I continued to push, hoping it was going to go from better to best very soon. The second year came, and as I had hoped, it was a big breakthrough for me. The profits that came in were perfect and satisfying. Three years later, I swerved and went into commerce.

Commerce was not as pretty sweet as expected. Even for someone like me, it was somehow tough. I was not the lazy type nor someone who gave up on things easily, but commerce was exhausting. It was paying, but not in the way I wanted considering how much I had put into it; what I was getting was nothing compared to what I was putting in. In my years as a businessman, I had learned when to get out of a failing business, and so I planned to leave commerce, but I was waiting for the right time. I began to regret quitting my first job, but it was too late, like waving to a plane in the air. I started thinking about new opportunities.

I attended business seminars and conferences, and it was in one of those gatherings that I heard something that roused me: "succeeding with your first try does not really prove that you are an entrepreneur, but when you fail and still bounce back stronger and better, then you can consider yourself an entrepreneur."

The saying got me thinking a lot, and so after some time I decided to venture into a transportation service. I discussed it with someone that I met at the seminar, and he bought the idea. Initially, it involved a great deal of capital outlay, but it was an easy project once I had a partner.

Now, we needed cars, but we didn't have enough money to get the number of vehicles we needed to start the business, so I came up with the idea of getting people to allow us to use their cars— the ones they left unused in their garages, which are still in good shape.

After lending these vehicles to us, the owners could later share the profit. The method worked well, as some families agreed that their cars would be better off in use than the garage. Eventually, we got twenty cars, and so we began the business. Things began to look good and so we increased the number of vehicles to forty and then to sixty.

However, we started having problems once we began to work with sixty cars; the drivers were no longer honest and maintaining the cars became a problem, and so we started missing orders. In fact, we were sued by two customers that missed their appointments. What actually made me back out was when we had the third case with the law, and this time it involved drugs.

I know danger when I see it; I used to be in the force and so I knew what could happen with an issue like this. The business lasted for two years.

I went into another business, this time a more complex and complicated firm. It was in the health service industry. At first, I was unsure and scared. Going into a health service was different and fifty times more serious than the previous businesses I'd tried. This time, it was not about selling home appliances or buying cars for transport services, it was actually saving human life. It was a big risk, one I was willing to take anyway. My wife was already in the system, and my kids were practicing to be in the field, so it was going to be a family business in the future.

The research I conducted this time was not like the kind I'd been doing. I spent so much time talking to everyone I could see who was already in the field. Personally, I underwent training for months. I knew how complicated this new business could be, and I knew that any simple mistake could cost someone's life and so I was not going to leave any stone unturned. I dug into every hole to get money, a lot of money. I made plans for everything I would be needing: office space, qualified workers, and so on. I had also set up a system to monitor the progress as everything went on. After I had learned about the requirements, skills, and every physical thing, I started to learn deeply about the laws regarding my proposed business. I came to know about various legal aspects protecting privacy and information about healthcare health insurance, such as the Health Insurance Portability and Accountability Act of 1996 (HIPPA).

Actually, I co-owned Family Healthcare Group, Inc. and Family Healthcare Services (DBA) with a Mr. Prince. But after some time, my spouse and I decided to break off and start our own health company. It was a risk, one whose uncertain outcome I doubted. However, I took the leap; my spouse and I resigned from Family Healthcare Group, Inc. and Mr. Prince took over, and thus came about the birth of Special Health Care, Inc. And so, after getting every necessary license, we began to work. It was something I could not believe.

When everything was prepared, I started employing workers. I made sure they were thoroughly screened by professionals. After that, I got the necessary equipment. I signed the documents required to get licensed, and having done that, work began in earnest. The next thing I did was to start marketing using a "paid referral" method. These tactics were the engine that boosted my business into the sky. I couldn't believe it—great numbers of clients flocked in every day. In just a little time, its positive development had broken the chart. The company grew so much that such success had never been recorded before in Houston or in Texas as a whole.

Now, the paid referral method helped me a lot, but it did something else; it caused ugly murmurings among my competitors. They were unhappy because a black newcomer was pushing them aside. They began to say many things. Soon, my friend in the force called me and told me about a series of allegations that had been filed against me. I was not very surprised, as I already knew something like that would happen soon. They filed suits claiming I used illegal means to steal their clients. I knew they'd find something with which to trap me, and so I called my lawyer and he told me to start preparing for a case.

I kept calm because I knew it was all going to land in the court, where I would be able to explain and also debunk every rumor that had been spread about me. The court was the only force that could beat me or free me, so why wait? Things were escalating, and so I called my family and explained how bad matters had gotten. They were scared, obviously, but I assured them everything was going to be fine. I was innocent and so were my workers; I made sure of that. From the beginning, I saw to it that everyone had a clean book. All this I did to block every angle my opponents might come from.

Yet, as I had expected, they finally found something with which to hold me; they finally showed up at my house.

Chapter Nine
THE MEDICARE
STRIKE TEAM

2 7th July, 2009: a day I would remember for the rest of my life. What I had dreaded now occurred. It was on a sunny Monday, and I was at home with my family when the Medicare Fraud Strike Force stormed my neighborhood. It was a scary scene as everyone scurried into their homes in fear. I could hear sirens blaring from every corner. Judging from the hostility, I could tell they came with full force. I knew they had come for me, but I didn't expect so much noise.

I was in the force, I knew what was happening, and I needed to brace myself for whatever was coming my way. I looked back and saw my wife holding the kids together, fighting back tears that flowed nonetheless down their cheeks.

"It's okay, babe, take the kids and wait for me inside."

Actually, I was scared too, but I had to be strong for them. I looked out through the window and saw that lots of SUVs, police vans, had surrounded my house. The hour had come. Quickly, I grabbed my phone and called my lawyer. I informed him about the ongoing rampage in my area, and he told me to get ready and follow them quietly. He was on his way too. But of course, I know what I must do; I must do as he said.

No sooner had I dropped the phone than I heard a knock on the door. I looked back, and my wife and kids were still there, crying profusely. The knock came again, and so I shifted to the door.

"Good evening, Mr. Clifford Ubani. I am Federal Agent Ross," the officer leading the raid announced immediately upon entering my house.

"Good evening, Officer Ross," I replied, trying hard to hide the nervousness in my voice.

"We are here to bring you in and to search your property," he said, displaying a search and arrest warrant to my face. "Come with me, Mr. Clifford, while the officers do their job."

I nodded and followed him. Several officers walked past us into the house as we made our way toward the vehicles parked outside.

Now, I was starting to get scared. I was sure my lawyer would be cooking something up, but still, despite how prepared I was it surprised me how terrified I felt. I still believed in justice, however, so I was not very bothered. As I was driven out of the neighborhood, I could see my wife and kids standing on the porch, watching. I was taken to the FBI office and kept in a waiting room.

I didn't know much about the Medicare Fraud Strike Force until they stormed my house. The US has set up different agencies to safeguard the health sector, seeing that anything and everything that concerns the welfare of citizens cannot be taken with light hands. Such task forces were set up by various acts to put things in order. Such was the Medicare Fraud Strike Force.

This strike force was first established in March, 2007 with the special focus of preventing and combating health care fraud, waste, and abuse as part of an effort to recover, generate, and outsource funds to finance the Affordable Healthcare Act, otherwise known as Obamacare, at a time when the administration was in desperate need to show the American people how it would be paid for.

In the United States, the first Office of Inspector General was established by an act of Congress in 1976 under the Department of Health and Human Services, to fight waste, fraud, and abuse in Medicare, Medicaid, and more than 100 other HHS programs. With approximately 1,600 employees, the OIG performs audits, investigations, and evaluations to establish policy recommendations for decision-makers and the public.

There are 73 federal offices of inspectors general, a significant increase since the statutory creation of the initial twelve offices by the Inspector General Act of 1978. The offices employ special agents—criminal investigators, often armed, and auditors. In addition, federal offices of inspectors general employ forensic auditors, evaluators, inspectors, administrative investigators, and a variety of other specialists to detect and prevent fraud or mismanagement of government programs and operations.

Office investigations may be internal, targeting government employees, or external, targeting grant recipients, contractors, or recipients of the various loans and subsidies offered through the thousands of federal domestic assistance programs. The Inspector General Reform Act of 2008 (IGRA) amended the 1978 act by increasing pay and various powers and creating the Council of the Inspectors General on Integrity and Efficiency (CIGIE).

In practice, the OIG develops and distributes resources to assist the health care industry in its efforts to comply with the nation's fraud and abuse laws and to educate the public about the fraudulent schemes so they can protect themselves and report suspicious activities. In recent years, the OIG has targeted hospitals and health care services for Stark Law and Anti-Kickback Statute violations pertaining to the management of physician compensation arrangements. In 2015, an announcement was issued to publicize the OIG's intent to regulate such non-compliance further.

In light of such efforts and consequent record-breaking settlements, health care experts have begun to call for the transition from paper-based physician time logging and contract management to automated solutions.

In the cell where I was kept at the FBI office, a million thoughts raced in my mind. I didn't know what was in store for me, so I was grateful that I had tied up every loose end. The cell was pretty cool and neat; I had been offered coffee twice, but I refused. I didn't want a coffee or tea or anything for that matter, I just want to speak to some-one. I always hated to find myself in a situation where I'm helpless.

After some time, a young officer walked into the room, a wicked grin across his face. I knew he had come to interrogate me. His fine suit and black shoes blazed in the dimly lit room. He was a federal agent. He cleared his throat as he pulled a chair for himself and sat facing me. He introduced himself , but I was too disturbed to listen. My mind was literally not in the room. He said some other things which I didn't pay attention to. There was only one thing I kept asking: why am I here?

Eventually, I got to know that I had been indicted on multiple counts of health care fraud and conspiracy resulting from my activity as CFO of the Family Healthcare Group, Inc., a company I co-owned with a business partner from June 2006 to October 2, 2008. I couldn't believe my ears; I thought I was going to scream! This was not the charge I was expecting. In fact, I was in no way involved in any fraudulent activity at any time.

I was shocked. I tried explaining things, but they were not ready to listen. I knew what was happening, but I still had faith in the court of law. I knew it was only the court that could get me out of this mess. I provided every point and fact to prove how strange the allegation filed against me was, but my attempt was abortive. My talk did no good, so I calmed down. My case was rushed in such a way that I could barely catch up with the things going on. Even the faith I had in the court was no more. I was denied a fair hearing. In short, it was a war, a lost one. My white lawyer asserted that I wouldn't be in the mess if I was a white man, and so it dawned on me that I had been caught in the snare of racism.

I was unjustly and arbitrarily rushed, then got indicted by the grand jury without regard to its own OIG internal safe guards that it accused me. I expected that the OIG would be smart enough to understand what it meant to go against its own standards and deny a citizen his rights. But that didn't mean anything to the agency. They blatantly failed to honor, or should I say ignored, their own internal rules, safeguards, and procedures established to assist the health care industry in complying with the nation's fraud and abuse laws. All of those standards and practices meant nothing to them.

I was clean and good; I was registered and certified by the TDAS, I underwent and passed stringent Medicare and Medicaid uidelines. I run a legal business; I was checked thoroughly and was approved. I had the necessary license and papers. My facilities were okay, I employed skilled and experienced personnel, and used durable medical equipment (DME) covered by Medicare. All these were the tests I passed, but the forces that I was battling with. were hell-bent on ruining me, and I didn't have that it would take to beat them. It was far worse than I had thought. I was losing.

The treatment I received showed that these guys really wanted me gone for good. I was not allowed to appear as a witness before the grand jury, nor was I given the privilege of a fair hearing. It was a setup, pure conspiracy. I was framed by people who were angry because a black man was beating them out of the race; they were mad because I was a problem for them.

Chapter Ten
NOSE DIVE

B y now, I had realized how deep I was in this mess. My efforts to quench every problem at a low level were futile. Things sped up to a pace I couldn't even comprehend. It was like I was swimming in a pool of injustice that had been prepared for me. I had no control over anything. It had all be planned out, from my arrest down to my prosecution. I didn't know much, nor did I understand all that was happening to me, so I made the move of hiring legal counsel to represent me in court.

On July 30, 2009, I hired the law firm of Scardino and Fazel. My hopes were high, but I was eventually disappointed. My attorney made little or no progress at all. It was a total waste of time. This new development was taking a terrible toll on kids, who were depressed and sad; in fact, it affected their studies. I continued to sign countless pieces of paperwork with my lawyer. After tons of futile talks every day, I would come home weak and sick. Even Special

Health Care, Inc. was dead. Things had gone from bad to worse now. After seven months, I began to look for different counsel to represent me. I had had enough of it with Fazel. On March 8, 2010, I hired a new attorney, A. Fisch.

By March 9, 2010, he filed a motion to the court to be my attorney. He had started making preparations in advance. He had handled lots of cases like my own, and so I decided his record made him was my best guy. He told me the agency would come at me through the court to offer a plea deal, which I must refuse. If the corrupt agency would use the court to hurt me, then the court was biased too. How then could I think it was safe to think I'd be cleared in the court?

If I accepted the plea deal, it meant I was pleading guilty to a crime I didn't commit. Fisch told me not to accept anything other than acquittal; the case was against the company, Family Healthcare Group, Inc., that allegedly violated the Civil Monetary Penalties Law provisions applicable to physician self-referrals, kickbacks, and false and fraudulent Claims. As a result, Family Healthcare Group, Inc. would have to settle it as self-disclosed conduct to OIG and agreed to pay back the amount as charged.

Fisch's advice proved that he knew what he was doing. Like he had said, the agency offered me a plea deal, which I turned down immediately. This angered and frustrated them. The look on the faces of the prosecuting counsel and the judge said it all; they expected me to jump at the deal so that they could end everything quickly. They wanted me gone, but it was not very easy for them at the moment.

The way I was being urged and pushed showed me what they were really up to, but I was ready for them. Me rejecting their plea deal thwarted their plans.

My new attorney's proposal to be my legal counselor was denied. I was shocked and confused. I had grown to believe that this man was going to help me; I had never heard of an attorney being denied the opportunity to represent his client. He called me and told me not to worry; he said it was just a matter of procedure. He must not have been sensing what I was sensing: even the court was biased! It was clear that I was losing. Once again, I was alone, but since I didn't know much, I continued to meet Fisch.

The denial of my new attorney looked very fishy, so it led me to do some research on my own. I went through the OIG false and fraudulent claims archive and found that there were 134 healthcare companies that allegedly violated the Civil Monetary Penalties Law provisions applicable to physician self-referrals, kickbacks, or false and fraudulent Claims from April 15, 2008, to June 22, 2011. It was surprising that none of the companies in question were criminally prosecuted. What the OIG did was to settle these cases as self-disclosed conduct and agreed to pay back (their companies) the amount as charged by their companies. On the other hand, for the same violation my spouse and I were criminally prosecuted and incarcerated, two different worlds in one country. The companies that walked away with their crimes were either owned by white Americans or co-owned by a white American.

On March 23, 2010, two Washington DC prosecutors, S. Sheldon and C. Reed, met with my former attorney. Apparently, they wanted me to accept the plea deal, so they had turned to the attorney I had fired long ago. Obviously, everything they were doing was off the book. Now, they were aware that I had fired Fazel, so why didn't meet my new attorney? The way I saw things, my former attorney was now with them and they were working hand in hand. I was sure they had deliberately rejected my new attorney's motion to be my attorney of record because they knew he wouldn't give in to them.

The plea deal stated that, if I accept the it, an additional case involving my spouse for her activity in Family Healthcare Group, Inc., where she had a brief stint of employment as Director of Nurses, would not be filed.

Nevertheless, my new attorney told me not to give in regardless of the threat. He said if I accepted the deal, it would mean I was walking right into their trap. He said I needed to be strong and wise at this point, as I could be forced to make a mistake that could jeopardize everything. I was aware that it was all one of their schemes to put me in a tight corner, since my wife was involved now and I would want her out of the entire mess. Certainly, I didn't want her involved, but at the same time, I was not ready to dance to the agency's tune.

Three months already in this fiasco and I still didn't have an approved attorney yet. I was confused. Even if I was guilty, I still had the right to hire an attorney to defend me during my trial. I met with some of my friends in the force, and when I told them of what I was going through, they were surprised that I had issues with the agency. I met with Fisch to see how things were progressing, but his motion was still being denied.

The agency told me they would file other charges against me if I didn't agree to the plea deal, but I was not scared or moved. I wouldn't go on my knees and confess to crimes I didn't commit. It was a funny struggle, actually; I knew my enemies, but I couldn't touch them. It seemed they wanted to break me down till I eventually accepted their offer, but my new attorney assured me that if I did, then I had lost the fight totally, and so I continued refusing, thinking their threat was just a bluff to scare me.

On July 2, 2010, the two prosecutors actually carried out their threat. They filed an additional charge against me, and they involved my spouse. Now, I had two separate cases in two different courts with two different judges respectively: case H-10-416 and case H-09-421, with the same charge in both courts. I was terrified this time. They had hit me really bad. I called my new attorney. I needed to act fast if I was going to free myself. I wanted my wife out at all costs too, but I had no options; it had gone from worse to worst. I remembered the words of Walter Savage Landor, "delay of justice is injustice."

Chapter Eleven
FROM WORSE TO WORST

❧

Finally, the day I was to make an appearance in court came. I still had no legal counselor to defend me. They were aware, since it was their scheme all along, so I was allowed to improvise and get a temporary arrangement. I hired Mr. Fry for just one court arraignment. On September 14, 2010, I got another attorney, Alston, for another sitting. I had high expectations for this new attorney, hoping he would be able to repel the plea deal that had been offered to me. I was trying to avoid a situation in which my wife and I would face prosecution at the same time. I was in a dilemma now with no good options before me. However, one thing was certain now; if I didn't accept the plea deal offered to me and still didn't have an attorney to help me win the case, then I would be sliding deeper into more trouble.

I was very distressed. My hands were slipping off whatever I held to steady myself in the rushing water of injustice; in fact, I was drowning already. I was worried about my kids, too, about what was going to become of them if things went the wrong way. If I was eventually sentenced to prison, I didn't want them to be alone in this ugly world, and the only way to prevent that from happening was to make sure my wife was off the hook, and the only way to do that was to accept the deal.

Accepting the deal meant I would admit that I was guilty to crimes I didn't commit, but my wife would be spared. It was a grave decision, but I was willing to take it for my kids. I didn't have anyone else in the US at that time; my cousin was somewhere else and the old woman whom I met on the plane remained a very dear friend to my family, but she had also left. During my time at a probation officer, I had seen what happens when kids are left alone by themselves, so I was not going to let it happen. I accepted the deal.

On September 29, 2010, less than two weeks after he had been hired, the new attorney, Alston, without good understanding of the case and what I was getting in return if I agreed to the guilty plea, rushed the whole process through. He made no serious attempt to retrieve the first deal offer. In a case of this magnitude with such far-reaching consequences on my life and family, the gap of three months in which I was without an attorney and adequate representation presented an opportunity for the prosecutors to force-feed me a plea bargain that was worse than a conviction, as events later revealed. All this under my legal counsel's watch. I would never have knowingly and willingly accepted a plea offer that was so contrary to my own interest, making my worst nightmare a reality. The new deal offer was worse than the first deal. As a matter of fact, there was no deal at all.

I didn't stop undertaking my own personal research. I made another important discovery in a document I found from the Secretary of State's Business Incorporation Department. The evidence was an official record in showing the actual date my spouse and I resigned from Family Healthcare Group, Inc. This date was twenty months before the alleged offense for which I and my wife were being arraigned in court.

On that day in court, considering everything I had seen and heard, I was sure I would be going to jail. I was scared and felt broken, but I had to be strong. I was in a mess where my only hope turned out to be my downfall, so I was beaten down hard. I thought about all the things that I would miss while I was behind bars, how I would be in a dark room during the time my kids were reaching every milestone in their lives.

The judge that delivered the verdict felt sorry for me. She knew it was not right, but her hands were tied too. The judge openly stated that if today's court appearance had not been for my sentencing, she would have given me another defense lawyer. All she could do at that point was to accept my new findings and evidence under oath as part of my court file recording in case I decide to appeal the case in the future. She added that my former attorney, Fisch, had a serious effect on the outcome of the case but nothing could be done now to correct the situation because it remained only an allegation until he was tried and convicted.

The judge further stated in her opinion per sentencing that, "If I were to give a personal opinion on the matter, I would say I sensed some form of injustice in the system and it was only bad that Mr. and Mrs. Clifford Ubani were subjected to the case." She added that "There is an injustice because Mr. Fisch said or did what's been alleged." From her words, I deduced something she didn't want to be quoted from her at a later date. There was something she wanted to change but didn't have the power to. Her actions and words suggested to me that she knew more than she said, but was only there to deliver her verdict.

However, I was sentenced to 108 and 87 months in prison concurrently. The announcement shocked me so much that I began to think I had prepared myself, enough but I hadn't. I secretly still wished a miracle would happen, but it never happened. But that was not the real shocker. I almost run mad when my wife was convicted, too. I couldn't believe it; the deal had been fake all along. She was sentenced to 97 months in prison, leaving our five young, vulnerable kids all alone by themselves.

I was shattered by the pronouncement on my wife. I took the deal mainly because I wanted to her to be with the kids. I felt sorry, I felt that I had brought her into the mess. My wife had been a registered nurse for twenty years and throughout her active practice, she had a very good employment history and no criminal record whatsoever. Her sentencing meant that she now had a permanent criminal record and she would have to forfeit her nursing license. That was like throwing away all that she had worked for and built from high school. Mr. Prince was also tried and sentenced to prison alongside his wife for the same crimes I and my wife were charged with. I called Kelvin and other persons that I could trust and asked them to help me look after my kids.

On October 19, 2010, a federal indictment on twenty-one counts, case H-11-722, was filed against the attorney Fisch and others for alleged conspiracy, obstruction of justice, and etc.. Several events had occurred under my nose. At a point I wondered if I was just a pawn in a bigger game. I was not aware that at approximately the same time that the Department of Justice in Washington D.C., represented by Mr. Sheldon and Reed, was busy prosecuting my case, another branch of the Department of Justice, the United States Attorney's Office in Houston, was also investigating my attorney Fisch and others for defrauding criminal defendants.

During their investigation, conversation with Fisch and others was intercepted. Rob was the prosecutor. My spouse and I debriefed with him a couple of times concerning our involvement with Attorney Fisch and others. As this was going on, the two branches of the DOJ were not communicating with each other. This invariably affected their decision-making and the outcome of our case. I was going to jail for two different trials to serve two different jail terms. The lack of communication between both prosecutors was highly unprofessional, and it was disgraceful that a court of that magnitude could not effectively do its job. Well, they refused to communicate with each other so that they would have enough excuse to carry out their mischief.

Chapter Twelve
THE END:
THE INCOMPLETE TRUTH

My wife and I have each spent four years in prison now. Those years have been rough and long, but we are strong. Fisch's trial was not concluded until June 2015. When it ended, he was convicted. Per Judge Atlas's comment, contained in the sentencing record, it's sad for Mr. & Mrs. Clifford Ubani, they're innocent, not guilty.. It was in jail that I learnt that Fisch had been sent to prison and that the presiding judge said that I was innocent. I was glad; the statement was a good report, one that was going to help my family. Fisch's trial paved a new and positive way for us.

One question I kept asking myself was about the client protection fund that every state in the US and provinces in Canada have in some form. In Texas, this fund is called the Client Security Fund and it holds more than $3 million. Payouts are funded through an annual appropriation from the Bar, interest on the balance, and any restitution received. Applications to the Fund are reviewed and acted upon by the Client Security Fund Subcommittee, a standing subcommittee of the State Bar's Board of Directors. The CDC, through Claire Reynolds, serves as the administrator and legal counsel to the Fund, and Reynolds is responsible for conducting investigations on applications and presenting recommendations to the Subcommittee.

Unless the lawyer is already disbarred, resigned in lieu of discipline, or deceased, eligible applicants must file a grievance which results in a finding that the lawyer stole the client's money or failed to refund an unearned fee. Applicants must present proof of their losses and meet the statute of limitations for the Fund, which is eighteen months following the date of the disciplinary judgment. I made my application for this client security fund, knowing very well that I was qualified to receive something from it. I paid $50, 000 to my attorney, who is a member of the state bar of Texas. The court did not allow him to represent me and did not give me any reason. Later the lawyer was indicted, tried, convicted, and sentenced to prison. When I applied for this client security fund, they told me that I was qualified to receive it since I went to prison without him representing me in court; instead he committed a crime and is now in prison.

Why shouldn't I get the $50,000 I paid the attorney from the client security fund which is intended for that purpose? It's simple: because I am different, a black man of Nigerian decent, and people who operate the client security fund are biased. The wheels of justice caught up with my personal attorney in the case. He was indicted by federal prosecutors, and one of the cases cited as part and parcel of his legal sins was mine, 4:10-CR-00416-001. He was tried and convicted. This brings us to the famous legal analogy of the fruits of a poisoned tree. If my personal attorney's legal sins were steeped in scarlet and legally unforgivable, then he represents a poisoned tree and everything he touched legally is considered contaminated.

After my former attorney Fisch was found guilty as alleged and sent to prison, I was returned to court after spending 65 months of my 108-month sentence in prison. For this court appearance, the presiding judge had been replaced by another who knew little or nothing about the case. An opportunity that would have helped to remind the judge about the comment the first judge had made, about our innocence, if Fisch was found guilty as charged. The system and the player knew the implication of that statement: they knew it would have automatically wiped the board clean for my wife and me. But the players in the whole controversial scandal refused for once to connect the dots. They blatantly refused to let the new presiding judge know what was said. I wondered if that was erased from the record that was given to the new presiding judge.

The unwillingness of the justice system and its operators to make this link to my spouse's serving a staggering sentence in prison kept me wondering if I was the target or my wife was. I wondered if I was actually the one they wanted out of their way or if they were particularly targeting my wife and I was the only link to getting her. I was freed, but my wife still remains in prison till this date. For her to get out of prison as I did, I need to hire a lawyer and file a motion to the court asking it to re-open her file and then wait. So, I need a lawyer and money to pay one, which I don't have at the moment.

As I regained my freedom, I imagined every day what my children were going through without us. I knew even though we were innocent, the fact that we were in prison and my wife is still in prison would be a stigma against them. My girls were quite emotional like their mother, but my boys had my kind of heart.

My former partner, Mr. Prince, remains in prison still. His wife was released before me. While in prison, I never gave up faith in my marketing strategy. I knew I wasn't in prison because of the strategy, I was in prison because of a failed system.

The four years I spent in prison should not be in vain. They afforded me the opportunity to engage in more research and review and to fine-tune the paid referral marketing model to create a Peer-to-Peer Referral Reward Contribution combined with a subscription business model to rewardingly monetize, engage, and enhance user experience across social networking platforms. Now I wish to put this business model, which has worked for me before, into a more refined form to better users' experience in social networking platforms around the world.

Appendix:
UNJUST VERDICTS

H ere is another painful story of injustice recorded in the United States system. Forty-six years ago, a teenage boy named Wilbert Jones was wrongly accused of rape. Not a single shred of physical evidence existed to prove his guilt. He also had a witness who provided an alibi proving he was somewhere else. He had nothing to do with it. Nothing at all. In fact, a serial rapist who had victimized another woman a few weeks later was the perpetrator. And the local police and prosecutors had evidence of this but decided to keep it to themselves. A full three months after the crime, the police couched the victim into identifying Wilbert as the man who raped her. And the jury convicted Wilbert Jones, a young teenager, for a horrible crime that he did not commit. From 1971 on, Wilbert suffered through an unthinkable prison sentence.

Think about this: when he was convicted, it was just two years after the assassination of the then-President. And all through the

70s, 80s, 90s, and 2000s until 2017, Wilbert Jones was in prison, spending a large part of his adulthood behind bars. For the record, Jones is black and poor; he was convicted after a trial lasting a few hours. On one uncertain eyewitness's testimony, he was sent away for what could have been the rest of his life.

Twenty-nine of the 30 freed clients under Innocence Project New Orleans were like Jones, young black men, arrested and convicted in trials that lasted less than one day. We know African Americans are disproportionately represented among the exoneree population nationwide. We should tend to ask why we accept a cursory and inaccurate process for the poor and black people. Here is where the divide sets in.

The police investigated the rape for which Wilbert was convicted by waiting for a name and putting him in a lineup. When the victim called the police to say she wasn't certain it was him, they did nothing more, but he eventually spent over 16,000 days in prison for a crime he did not commit. Here several matters arise: Why aren't the police and enforcement agents given adequate resources to conduct an effective and thorough investigation? Also, how can they be enabled with modern best practices in eyewitness identification procedures? We should also ask about the value placed on the lives we ruin when people are wrongly imprisoned. Ultimately, the current answers to these questions paint the picture of a broken legal system.

Another tragedy was the death of Kalief Browder at just twenty-two years of age. This came after he spent three years in jail without ever being convicted of the crime with which he was charged. Kalief's story is of great concern not just to his family, but the entire community of New York.

The events surrounding his conviction and death clearly depict a deeply broken justice system in the United States. The system punishes people because they are poor and helpless, subjecting them to coldhearted and brutal dealings. Kalief was arrested in 2010. As at that time, he was just sixteen years of age and was basically accused of stealing a backpack. From there, he was additionally charged with robbery, grand larceny, and assault. His bail was set at $3,000.

His family could not afford that amount. Consequently, Kalief didn't get to go home after he was charged. Instead, he was sent to a jail in New York City. All this was because he was wrongly accused and he could not afford to pay $3,000. Kalief spent more than 1,100 days incarcerated, maintaining his innocence throughout. Prosecutors repeatedly offered plea deals, which Kalief rejected. After 74 days of incarceration, bail was revoked altogether. Moreover, this poor boy was falsely and unjustly accused of stealing.